You are the
Light of the World

Magical Mantras for Children

Wendy Quintero Navarro

Illustrated by Stefanie Geyer

Balboa Press books may be ordered through booksellers or by contacting:

Balboa Press
A Division of Hay House
1663 Liberty Drive
Bloomington, IN 47403
www.balboapress.com
844-682-1282

Because of the dynamic nature of the Internet, any web addresses or links contained in this book may have changed since publication and may no longer be valid. The views expressed in this work are solely those of the author and do not necessarily reflect the views of the publisher, and the publisher hereby disclaims any responsibility for them.

Any people depicted in stock imagery provided by Getty Images are models, and such images are being used for illustrative purposes only.
Certain stock imagery © Getty Images.

ISBN: 979-8-7652-3853-0 (sc)
ISBN: 979-8-7652-3862-2 (hc)
ISBN: 979-8-7652-3852-3 (e)

Library of Congress Control Number: 2023901629

Print information available on the last page.

Balboa Press rev. date: 03/02/2023

BALBOA.PRESS
A DIVISION OF HAY HOUSE

Dedicated to

My husband, Renato,

Thank you for your love and support on this journey.
My inner light shines brighter by your side.

My son, Maximiliano,

For being my guiding light into this magical
world. May you always shine your light
to the world. Mommy loves you.

All children are wonderful and shine a unique light from within. You, yes you, are amazing and special in your own way. What is it that makes you who you are? Everything about you makes you extraordinary, especially what you feel inside your heart and the rest of your body.

Together, let's say some magical mantras that will help you shine your light brighter. A glowing, sparkling light will come from deep in your heart and illuminate your body.

⭐ I am Love

Love is that bubbly feeling that you get inside you when everything is just perfect. Close your eyes, place your hands on your heart, feel, and say deep in your heart,

"I am love. I am love. I am love."

Now turn to the person next to you, look them in the eyes, smile, and say, "I love you." And then give them a big, strong hug.

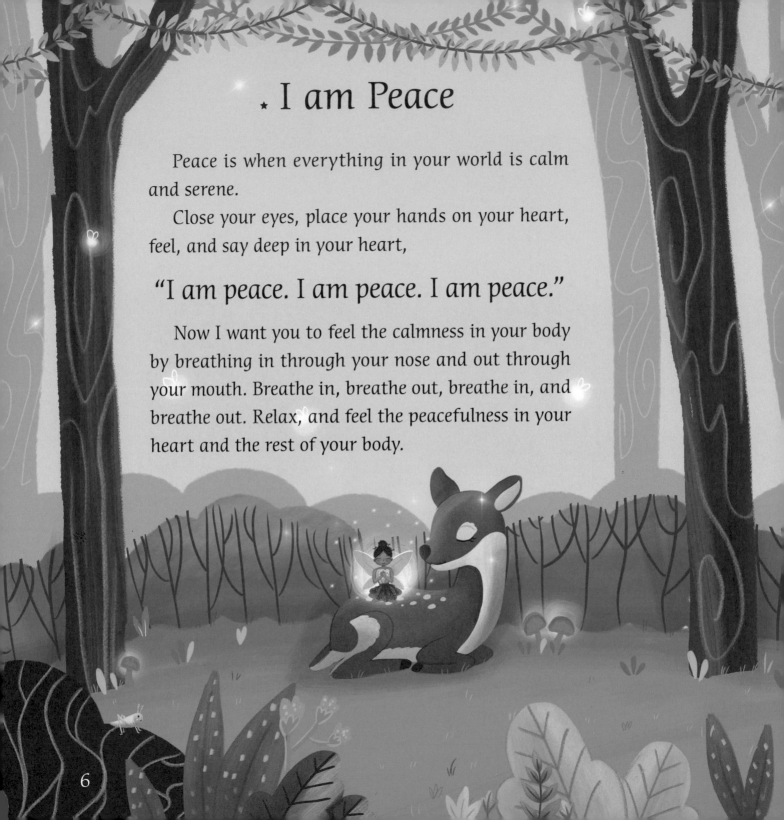

⋆ I am Peace

Peace is when everything in your world is calm and serene.

Close your eyes, place your hands on your heart, feel, and say deep in your heart,

"I am peace. I am peace. I am peace."

Now I want you to feel the calmness in your body by breathing in through your nose and out through your mouth. Breathe in, breathe out, breathe in, and breathe out. Relax, and feel the peacefulness in your heart and the rest of your body.

⭐ I am Joy

Joy is when you feel super happy and blissful about everything.

Close your eyes, place your hands on your heart, feel, and say deep in your heart,

"I am joy. I am joy. I am joy."

Now smile really big, get up on your feet, and jump all around like you did the most amazing thing. Yes, you did it!

⋆ I am Confident

Confidence is when you feel like you are on top of the world and can do and say anything.

Close your eyes, place your hands on your heart, feel, and say deep in your heart,

"I am confident. I am confident. I am confident."

Now imagine you are in a room. Stand up, and with your loudest voice, sing and dance your favorite song. You look confident from head to toe!

★ I am Beautiful

Being beautiful means that you are perfect just the way you are and look. Close your eyes, place your hands on your heart, feel, and say deep in your heart,

"I am beautiful. I am beautiful. I am beautiful."

Go to the mirror, look into your eyes, and say, "I am beautiful." Yes, you are! Do this every morning and every night, and see the beauty flow around you.

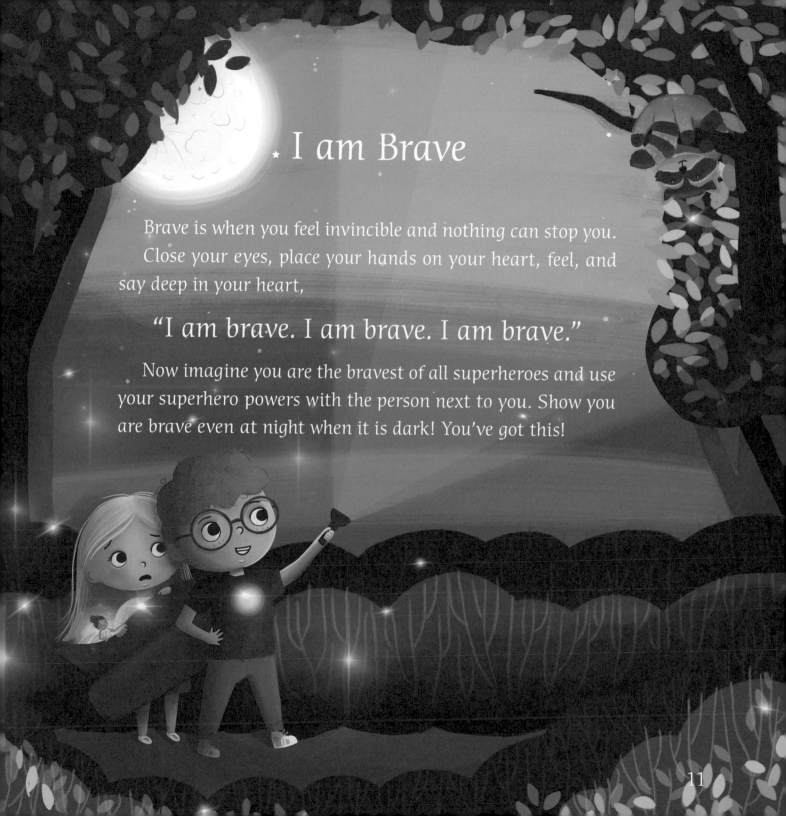

I am Brave

Brave is when you feel invincible and nothing can stop you. Close your eyes, place your hands on your heart, feel, and say deep in your heart,

"I am brave. I am brave. I am brave."

Now imagine you are the bravest of all superheroes and use your superhero powers with the person next to you. Show you are brave even at night when it is dark! You've got this!

⭐ I am Strong

Strong is when you feel that no matter how big or small you are, you can do anything.

Close your eyes, place your hands on your heart, feel, and say deep in your heart,

"I am strong. I am strong. I am strong."

Now imagine you have the biggest muscles in the world and you can move and pick up anything. Wow! Look at your muscles!

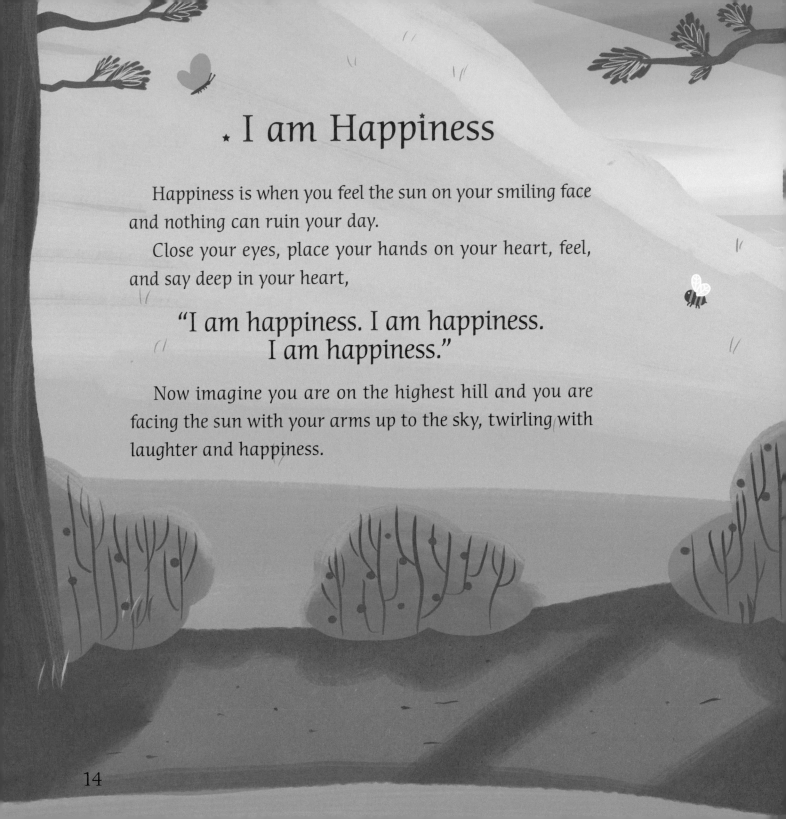

⋆ I am Happiness

Happiness is when you feel the sun on your smiling face and nothing can ruin your day.

Close your eyes, place your hands on your heart, feel, and say deep in your heart,

"I am happiness. I am happiness. I am happiness."

Now imagine you are on the highest hill and you are facing the sun with your arms up to the sky, twirling with laughter and happiness.

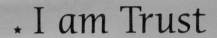

⭑ I am Trust

Trust is when you listen to a part of yourself inside your heart and the rest of your body. It's a part of you that always knows the answer and is guiding you.

Close your eyes, place your hands on your heart, feel, and say deep in your heart,

"I am trust. I am trust. I am trust."

Now tell a friend to pick a number from one to five in their mind, then guess the number. You are an amazing mind reader!

⋆ I am Safe

Safe is when you feel in control even though there can be lots of things going on around you that you don't understand and might seem confusing in such a grown-up world.

Close your eyes, place your hands on your heart, feel, and say deep in your heart,

"I am safe. I am safe. I am safe."

Now hold the person's hand next to you and tell them what you did today. As they listen, know that you are loved and safe.

⋆ I am Grateful

Gratitude is when you are thankful for everything and everyone in your life. Close your eyes, place your hands on your heart, feel, and say deep in your heart,

"I am grateful. I am grateful. I am grateful."

Now go to everyone in your house and say, "Thank you for being you," even your pets! Then go to everything in your room and say, "Thank you" too.

⭐ I am Forgiveness

Forgiveness is when you say sorry to people you hurt through your words or actions. It is also when they say sorry for hurting your feelings too.

Close your eyes, place your hands on your heart, feel, and say deep in your heart,

"I am forgiveness. I am forgiveness. I am forgiveness."

Now turn to the person next to you, place your hands on your heart, and tell them that you forgive them. Then ask if they will forgive you. Just saying it is perfect practice.

19

⋆ I am Compassion

Compassion is when you know how someone else is feeling and you are willing to be a friend.

Close your eyes, place your hands on your heart, feel, and say deep in your heart,

"I am compassion. I am compassion. I am compassion."

Now with the person next to you, talk about a time when you saw someone who was feeling sad or angry. Talk about how you can be a friend, and help them feel better and happier.

20

I am Empowerment

Empowerment is when you feel this power inside you building up to do something good for yourself and for others.

Close your eyes, place your hands on your heart, feel, and say deep in your heart,

"I am empowered. I am empowered. I am empowered."

Now imagine you can do anything yourself like tie your shoes, get dressed, and brush your teeth. You are so independent!

★ I am Unique

Unique is when you know that you are special and there is no one like you in the world.

Close your eyes, place your hands on your heart, feel, and say deep in your heart,

"I am unique. I am unique. I am unique."

Now talk to the person next to you about a time when you did something different from someone else. It is perfectly fine to be unique. This is what makes you different in your own way.

23

⋆ I am Light

Light is when you feel this energy growing and glowing inside your heart and it expands all around you.

Close your eyes, place your hands on your heart, feel, and say deep in your heart,

"I am light. I am light. I am light."

Now imagine you are a shining star and put your hands on your heart. Close your eyes, and see a light coming from the sky to the top of your head, through your body, and out the bottom of your feet into the earth. Then bring that bright light inside your heart, out, and all around your body.

You are the light of the world.

Now go out and shine your light to the world!
Remember that all children are magnificent and there is only one of *you* full of these wonderful, magical mantras within your heart.

About the Author

Wendy Quintero Navarro is a mother,
wife, and educator with a master's degree and
teaching credential in education. As a mother
and educator, she understands the importance of
affirmations and how it helps children embody who
they are meant to be. She believes it is imperative
to teach children to be strong, independent, and
loving human beings. This empowerment
can then evolve as they grow up from
childhood to adulthood to shape a
better future for the world.

Printed in the United States
by Baker & Taylor Publisher Services